Every Kid's Guide to
Being a
Communicator

Written by
JOY BERRY

CHILDRENS PRESS ®
CHICAGO

About the Author and Publisher

Joy Berry's mission in life is to help families cope with everyday problems and to help children become competent, responsible, happy individuals. To achieve her goal, she has written over two hundred self-help books for children from infancy through age twelve. Her work has revolutionized children's publishing by providing families with practical, how-to, living skills information that was previously unavailable in children's books.

Joy has gathered a dedicated team of experts, including psychologists, educators, child developmentalists, writers, editors, designers, and artists to form her publishing company and to help produce her work.

The company, Living Skills Press, produces thoroughly researched books and audiovisual materials that successfully combine humor and education to teach children subjects ranging from how to clean a bedroom to how to resolve problems and get along with other people.

Managing Editor: Ellen Klarberg
Copy Editor: Kate Dickey
Contributing Editors: Jean Buckley, Nancy Cochran, Barbara Detrich, Frank Elia, Bob Gillen, Kathleen McBride, Susan Motycka, Gary Passarino
Editorial Assistant: Sandy Passarino

Art Director: Laurie Westdahl
Design: Abigail Johnston, Laurie Westdahl
Production: Abigail Johnston, Caroline Rennard
Illustrations designed by: Bartholomew
Inker: Linda Hanney
Colorer: Linda Hanney
Composition: Curt Chelin

You are a communicator. You communicate every day with everyone around you. You communicate in many ways.

In **EVERY KID'S GUIDE TO BEING A COMMUNICATOR**, you will learn the following:

- what communication is,
- how you communicate with your body,
- how you communicate through various kinds of art,
- how you communicate with words, and
- how to communicate what you want to communicate.

Communication is exchanging or sharing feelings, thoughts, or information.

A *communicator* is a person who exchanges or shares feelings, thoughts, or information.

You are a communicator. You communicate in many ways.

Sometimes you use your **head** to communicate. Your head can communicate, "Yes." It can also communicate, "No."

Sometimes you use your *face* to communicate.
Your face can communicate, "I'm happy."
It can also communicate, "I'm sad."

Your face can communicate, "I'm mad."
It can also communicate, "I'm annoyed and
frustrated."

Your face can communicate, "I'm thinking."
It can also communicate, "I'm confused."

Your face can communicate, "I'm surprised."
It can also communicate, "I'm worried."

Your face can communicate, "I'm scared."
It can also communicate, "I'm disappointed."

Sometimes you use your **hands** to communicate.
Your hands can say, "No."
They can also say, "OK."

Your hands can say, "I hope so."
They can also say numbers.

Your hands can say, "Shhh...that's too loud."
Your hands can also say, "I can't hear."

Sometimes you use your **arms and hands** to communicate.

Your arms and hands can say, "Hello."

They can also say, "Good-bye."

Your arms and hands can say, "Right here."
They can also say, "Over there."

Your arms and hands can say, "You!"
They can also say, "Me!"

Your arms and hands can say, "Give it to me."
They can also say, "Take it."

Your arms and hands can say, "Come here."
They can also say, "Stay away."

Your arms and hands can say, "I don't know."
They can also say, "I won."

Your arms and hands can say, "You did a good job. I like what you did!"
They can also say, "Congratulations!" or "Let's be friends."

Sometimes you use your *whole body* to communicate.

Your body can say, "I'm shy. Leave me alone."

It can also say, "I feel rejected and alone."

Your body can say, "I'm confident. I know I can do it!"

It can also say, "I'm proud of myself. I like the things I do."

Your body can say, "I love you."

Your body can also say, "I hate you."

Sometimes you might want to communicate through various kinds of *art.*

Art can often communicate thoughts and feelings that are not easily communicated with words. You can communicate through the arts of *painting, drawing, sculpture,* and *photography.*

You can communicate through the art of *music*.

You can communicate through the art of *dance* or *body movement.*

You can communicate through the art of *writing*.

You can communicate through the art of *speech.*

You can communicate through the art of *drama*.

Sometimes you communicate by *talking*. When you talk, you use *words*.

Sometimes you need only one word to communicate.

Sometimes you use more than one word to
communicate.

The same words can communicate different messages.

The meaning you give to words depends upon many things, such as how **loudly** or how **softly** you say them.

The meaning you give to words depends upon how *slowly* or how **quickly** you say them.

The meaning you give to words also depends upon how *kindly* or how *unkindly* you say them.

The meaning you give to words depends upon how *sincerely* or how *insincerely* you say them.

The meaning you give to words also depends upon how *confidently* or how *timidly* you say them.

The meaning you give to words depends on how *enthusiastically* or how *unenthusiastically* you say them.

The meaning you give to words also depends on
what you are doing when you say them.

You need to follow three rules when you want to communicate important messages such as

- how you feel,
- what you think,
- what you want,
- what you need,
- your hopes or dreams, or
- facts and information.

1. Communicate to the right people.

As much as possible, avoid communicating with people who are *not* interested in you or what you have to say.

Instead, communicate with people who *are* interested in you and what you have to say.

2. Choose the right time to communicate.

Avoid communicating when you or the other person is too busy to think about what you have to say.

Instead, communicate at a time when both you and the other person can pay attention to what you have to say.

3. Communicate accurately and honestly.

Communicate your thoughts and feelings truthfully.

Only when you communicate accurately and honestly can people know and understand what you want them to know.

Only when you communicate accurately and honestly can people respond accurately and honestly to you.

You are a communicator.

You communicate in many ways.

When you want to communicate important messages, it is important that you communicate

- to the right people,
- at the right time, and
- in the right way.